COMPOSTING AND GARDENING

BY ROBIN TWIDDY

One SMALL STEP for kids

One giant leap towards SAVING the WORLD!

BookLife PUBLISHING

©2021
BookLife Publishing Ltd.
King's Lynn
Norfolk, PE30 4LS

All rights reserved.
Printed in Malta.

A catalogue record for
this book is available from
the British Library.

ISBN: 978-1-83927-847-1

Written by:
Robin Twiddy

Edited by:
Madeline Tyler

Designed by:
Drue Rintoul

PHOTO CREDITS

Images are courtesy of Shutterstock.com. With thanks to Getty Images, Thinkstock Photo and iStockphoto. 4&5 – Asier Romero, Ugis Riba, Hung Chung Chih, Ambartsumian Valery, Rich Carey, Alexey Laputin, Toa55. 6&7 – Mountain Brothers. 8&9 – Asier Romero, VDWimages, Roman Mikhailiuk, Neil Mitchell, ssuaphotos. 10&11 – Al fred, Rawpixel.com, Alex East, Ms.Karyn, Leena Robinson. 12&13 – Asier Romero, Anton P Daskalov, Dad's Shots, Laurence Berger, Erik dam. 14&15 – Asier Romero, Pinkyone, Steve Mann. 16&17 – kaband, Lightspring, sirikorn thamniyom, LianeM, KingTa, Goldution. 18&19 – Prostock-studio, Delovely Pics, Thicha6327, Asier Romero, ronstik. Marquisphoto. 20&21 – Luminis, DuleS, Dmitrijs Dmitrijevs, Ioannis Pantzi, Roman Samborskyi, Sarah Marchant, Bozena Fulawka. 22&23 – Krakenimages.com, Asier Romero, jgolby, Vadym Zaitsev, 135pixels, Ton Weerayut Photographer. 24&25 – Asier Romero, DreamHack, Kevin Day, Gorlov-KV, Toey Toey, HollyHarry, dave_liza. 26&27 – Asier Romero, Monkey Business Images, kryzhov, AnnGaysorn. 28&29 – Brocreative, Ink Drop. 30 – Asier Romero.

CONTENTS

Words that look like this are explained in the glossary on page 31.

You can (help) Save the World

The world is in trouble and it needs your help! It needs everyone's help. No one can save the world on their own, but together we can make a change. Our planet is facing many challenges, and lots of these are because of humans. The climate crisis is a big problem. We can see how humans have made it worse by looking at changes in the weather, the oceans and the air we breathe.

ROBIN TWIDDY PRESENTS:

SMALL STEPS REVOLUTIONARIES

Formed to save the world, the **Small Steps Revolution** gains new members every day!

Watch with amazement as the **Small Steps Revolutionaries** save the world one small step at a time!

Featuring Brenda – the Composting and Gardening revolutionary!

These are the Small Steps Revolutionaries. They are changing the world one step at a time. Whether it's being energy efficient or learning how to compost, eating locally or living zero waste, recycling or using water wisely, no problem is too big or too small for this band of heroes. By the time you finish this book you too will be a member of the Small Steps Revolution. Strap in, recruit – it's time to save the world!

Grow Your Knowledge

The first step to becoming a Small Steps Revolutionary is growing your knowledge. This means learning as much as you can about the change you want to see. There are lots of ways to grow your knowledge. Here are some places to get started.

Learn from others – do you know anyone who knows a lot about gardens and gardening? Ask them about it.

Visit the library – ask the librarian to help you find books about the environment.

"Knowledge is power – arm yourself!"

"Only if we understand, can we care. Only if we care, we will help. Only if we help, we shall be saved."
– Jane Goodall

Jane Goodall is a conservationist who studies apes and works to protect them.

"Those who do not learn from history are doomed to repeat it!"

Theodore Roosevelt was the 26th President of the United States.

"People don't care how much you know until they know how much you care."
– Theodore Roosevelt

Check your local council's website to find out about composting services in your area.

Research online – there are lots of great websites about gardening and composting.

SMALL STEP: GROW YOUR KNOWLEDGE!

Use an online <u>carbon dioxide</u> (CO_2) calculator to find out what your carbon footprint is. (Find out more about your carbon footprint on page 9.)

Knowledge is important but make sure that the information you look at is accurate. A good way to do that is to see who else agrees, writes or talks about the same information. Has it come from a <u>reliable</u> place or person?

A Home-Grown Revolution

Brenda is a Small Steps Revolutionary. Being a Small Steps Revolutionary means making small changes in your own life to help make a global change and inspire others to do the same.

Pollution made by people has caused lots of damage to nature and our environment. I want to do something about it. That's why I joined the SMALL STEPS REVOLUTION!

I work in my garden as a way of taking **Small Steps** to help nature. Some of the things I do help me lower my carbon footprint.

CARBON FOOTPRINT

Your carbon footprint is the amount of CO_2 created through the things you do. This includes the things you buy and throw away. There are so many ways that we add to our carbon footprint that we don't think about or see.

THE HIDDEN THREAT!

Here are some of the surprising ways we add to our carbon footprint:

When we use electricity, we are adding to our carbon footprint.

Generating electricity in power stations produces CO_2.

When we travel by car.

The fumes from cars have greenhouse gases in, and this adds to our carbon footprint.

When we send food to landfill, we add to our carbon footprint.

When we put things in the bin, it is sent to landfill where it is buried in the ground. As organic waste rots in landfills, it creates lots of CO_2 and another greenhouse gas called methane.

SMALL STEP: MEASURE YOUR CARBON FOOTPRINT

There is a better way to get rid of organic waste that makes much less CO_2 – read about it on page 16.

Why Are Plants Important?

CO$_2$ is a greenhouse gas. Greenhouse gases affect the climate crisis by gathering in the __atmosphere__ where they make it harder for heat to leave the planet.

Our entire planet is one big __system__ made up of lots of different parts that all work together. Plants have an important job in this system. They take in CO$_2$ and release oxygen. People and animals breathe in oxygen and need it to live. The more we can help the trees and plants, the more we help the planet.

This is why the Amazon rainforest, a place full of trees, is often called the lungs of the planet.

Planting trees is a great *Small Step* you can take. If you can't plant a tree yourself, there are lots of charities that can plant one for you.

HABITATS

Plants are also homes and food for animals and insects. Humans are destroying them through pollution and by cutting them down to build on the land and turn it into farmland.

An animal's home is called its habitat.

Many animals are losing their habitats because their homes are being pulled down to be turned into farmland. One animal that is losing its home in this way is the orangutan. Orangutans need thick forests to survive. As these habitats disappear, so do the orangutans and the other wildlife that live there.

We need to do everything we can to protect our wildlife and nature. This is the reason that the Small Steps Revolution was started.

SMALL STEP: GROW PLANTS FOR THE ANIMALS IN YOUR GARDEN

Animal Homes

GARDENING TO HELP ANIMALS

How can we help animals in our gardens? As a **Small Steps Garden Revolutionary,** I do my best to garden in a way that helps local wildlife. Here are a few ways that you can support wildlife in your garden.

NATIVE PLANTS

Native plants are plants that have always grown in an area and haven't been brought there by people. Native plants are good for local wildlife. Find out what plants are native to your area and grow some in your garden.

BIRD BOXES AND BIRD TABLES

Build or buy a bird box or bird table for your garden. This will encourage lots of birds to visit.

Here are some important tips for your bird box:

- Make sure that it is sheltered and out of reach of other animals.
- Place it near a thick bush – small birds love to dash out of the bushes to feed safely.
- Put out different feed for different times of the year.
  - Put out fat balls in spring – this is good for when birds are feeding their young.
  - Put out seeds in winter.

BUG HOTEL

A good healthy garden needs good healthy insects. Building a bug hotel isn't hard. It can be really fun and will be a place for all the insects and spiders in your garden to live.

Choose a spot in your garden and pile up rocks, sticks, soil and rotting wood and leaves. Make sure that you leave lots of gaps and nooks for the insects to get in.

POND

All animals need fresh water, and having a pond in your garden gives animals a great place to drink. If you don't have enough space for a big pond, you could dig a hole and bury a bucket or plant pot in the ground. Fill this with rainwater.

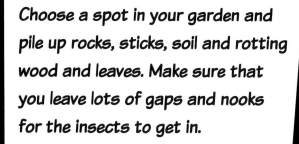

Grow _edible_ plants.

SMALL STEP: ADD BIRD BOXES, BUG HOTELS AND PONDS TO YOUR GARDEN

If you can't bury your pond, make sure there are rocks and sticks next to it for animals to climb up on.

Gardening in an Eco-Friendly Way

Being a **Small Steps Revolutionary** in the garden is more than just planting the right plants and providing shelter and food for animals. You need to think about how you garden. I call this **green gardening**.

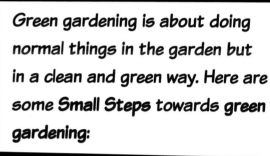

GREEN GARDENING

Green gardening is about doing normal things in the garden but in a clean and green way. Here are some **Small Steps** towards green gardening:

- Use organic <u>pesticides</u> to protect your plants.
  - When things are organic, it means they are natural and don't contain harmful <u>chemicals</u> that could harm the environment.
- Use baking soda and potassium bicarbonate in your soil.
  - This will <u>enrich</u> your soil and protect your flowerbeds from <u>pests</u> and weeds.
- If you want to have lights in your garden, choose solar-powered lights.
  - They will collect energy from the Sun during the day to power them at night.

There are a lot of plants that people call weeds and remove from their gardens. Even though they may not be as pretty as some other plants, they are actually very important. Lots of insects and animals eat weeds or make their homes in them.

Many different types of butterflies lay their eggs on nettles, which are weeds.

A Small Step you can take in your garden right now is to choose a patch to let weeds grow. You don't have to let them grow everywhere.

SMALL STEPS:
• USE ORGANIC PESTICIDES
• GROW SOME WEEDS

How and Why Should I Compost?

WHAT IS COMPOSTING?

Composting is when you put lots of organic waste together to rot. I know that sounds disgusting, but it isn't if you do it in the right way. All natural things break down and when they do they make <u>nutrients</u> which can help other living things such as plants grow.

Organic waste includes things such as garden waste, food waste and paper.

WHY SMALL STEPS REVOLUTIONARIES COMPOST

If we send our food and garden waste to landfill, it breaks down in a different way to how it does in a compost heap. When organic waste breaks down in landfill, it gives off lots of methane and CO_2.

Composting your kitchen food waste will take you one **Small Step** closer to **Living Zero Waste**. Check out my book to learn more about it!

Grant the Zero Waste Revolutionary

MAKE YOUR OWN COMPOSTER

1. Find somewhere in the shade that is around one metre long and one metre across.
2. Lay down some soil.
3. Start adding layers of brown waste and green waste.
4. Make sure the layers are between five and eight centimetres deep.
5. When you have finished layering your waste, finish with a layer of brown waste on top.

It is good to cover your compost heap with a tarpaulin if you can. This keeps the rain off and keeps your compost dry.

TARPAULIN ↗

GREEN WASTE

- Weeds
- Vegetable waste from the kitchen
- Grass cuttings

BROWN WASTE

- Wood chippings
- Sticks and twigs
- Straw
- Cardboard
- Paper
- Dead leaves

Turn your pile once a month. To do this, use a garden fork to move the compost around and let some air in.

SMALL STEP: COMPOST YOUR ORGANIC WASTE

Water in the Garden

Another part of being a **Small Steps Revolutionary** is using water wisely. This means saving water where you can, and only using the water you need without wasting any. This is just as important in the garden as it is in the house. My friend Ron is an expert in using water wisely.

Thanks, Brenda. The first thing to know is that the water from your tap has to come from somewhere. It comes from lakes and underground springs. If we use up too much water, these start to run out and the <u>quality</u> of water gets worse.

It is important that we think about how we use water – these lakes and springs are home to lots of wildlife.

The first **Small Step** to take is to set up something to catch rainwater. Rainwater is great for watering plants, and it means you don't have to run the tap. You can set up a water butt to collect water from your home's guttering, or you could use a large bucket or plant pot that sits out in the rain.

OTHER WAYS TO BE WATER WISE

Here are some other tips on saving water in your garden...

*Learn more about **Being Wise with Water** in my book.*

Use Grey water: Grey water is the old, used water from your house, such as bathwater, water leftover from cooking and even water from your washing up – if it isn't too soapy. Don't worry, your plants won't mind secondhand water.

Mulch Your Flowerbeds: This means laying down a layer of bark or straw on the soil. The mulch stops water from <u>evaporating</u> from the soil and means that you need to water your flowers less often.

SMALL STEPS:
• **COLLECT RAINWATER**
• **MULCH FLOWERBEDS**
• **USE GREY WATER TO WATER PLANTS**

If you take these **Small Steps**, you will be one giant leap closer to Being Wise with Water in the garden.

Buying into a Better Future

PUSH POWER!

Mowing the lawn doesn't need to be noisy and bad for the planet. Revolutionise the way you mow the lawn with *PUSH POWER!!!!*

SILENT!

FREE EXERCISE!

NO CO$_2$!

ENTER THE *AMAZING* WORLD OF

CRESS PETS®

OWN A TRAY OF CRESS-Y GOODNESS — *JUST ADD WATER!*

ALL YOU NEED IS A CONTAINER (AN OLD YOGHURT POT WILL DO), SOME COTTON WOOL, KITCHEN ROLL, CRESS SEEDS AND SOME WATER.

INSTRUCTIONS:
1. PUT YOUR DAMP KITCHEN ROLL AT THE BOTTOM OF YOUR POT.
2. PLACE SOME COTTON WOOL ON TOP OF THAT.
3. SPRINKLE YOUR SEEDS OVER THE COTTON WOOL.
4. NOW PLACE ON A WINDOWSILL AND WATCH IT GROW*

*CRESS GROWS FAST BUT NOT FAST ENOUGH THAT YOU WILL SEE IT GROW BEFORE YOUR EYES, SO DO NOT SIT AND WATCH YOUR CRESS UNLESS YOU ARE THE KIND OF KID WHO LIKES TO WATCH PAINT DRY!

Eggs—actly
What Your Garden Needs

If your soil needs a bit of a recharge, try spreading crushed up eggshells in the soil.*

Need to give your soil a bit of a helping hand?

Grab your eggs and get cracking!

*EGGSHELLS ARE NOT MAGIC. EGGSHELLS CONTAIN NUTRIENTS THAT ARE GOOD FOR THE SOIL.

HARNESS THE POWER OF EGGS!!!

FREE WATER

Top scientists have discovered a place to get free water and you won't guess where from. **THE SKY!**

Now, for the first time ever, you can collect your own rainwater to feed your plants. All you need is a bucket or water butt left outside when it rains.

THE SMALL STEPS REVOLUTION NEEDS YOU!

CALLING ALL KIDS. IT IS TIME TO MAKE A DIFFERENCE. DO YOU HAVE WHAT IT TAKES TO JOIN THE **SMALL STEPS REVOLUTION**? YOU **CAN** MAKE A DIFFERENCE! TO BECOME A MEMBER, SIMPLY TAKE ONE OF THE **SMALL STEPS** IN THIS BOOK, TAKE SOME PICTURES AND SHARE THEM WITH THE HASHTAG **#SMALLSTEPSREVOLUTION**

Grow Your Own

Another amazing **Small Step** you can take in your garden is to grow your own food. The food that we buy has its own carbon footprint. Growing lots of fruit and vegetables on large farms and then moving them to supermarkets uses lots of energy and <u>resources</u>, not to mention all the packaging. You can avoid some of these costs to the planet if you grow some of your food yourself.

Emilie the Eating Locally Revolutionary

That is right, Brenda. I am Emilie, and I am an expert in **Eating Locally**, and you can't get much more local than your own garden. By growing your own vegetables, you can cut down on the amount you buy and cut down on your carbon footprint.

Start off small. Pick one or two vegetables that you like and try growing them in your garden. My favourites to grow are courgettes, carrots and tomatoes.

COURGETTES

- Plant in early spring
- <u>Harvest</u> around ten weeks later
- Can plant in the ground, large containers or grow bags

CARROTS

- Plant between spring and summer
- Harvest around 12 to 16 weeks after planting
- Can be planted in the ground or a large pot

TOMATOES

- Plant in mid-spring
- Harvest around 12 weeks after planting
- Can be grown in the ground, large pots or grow bags

There is nothing better than eating food made from vegetables you have grown yourself.

If you want to start off smaller, have a go at growing your own herbs. Basil is a great place to start.

SMALL STEP:
GROW YOUR OWN
VEGETABLES

Good luck growing, recruits.

Upcycling in the Garden

All **Small Steps Revolutionaries** try to reduce the amount of waste and pollution they make. One of the best ways to do this is to <u>upcycle</u>. My friend Morrison is an expert in **upcycling**. I will let him show you how you can improve your gardening with **upcycling**.

Upcycling is when you give an old or broken thing a new purpose. I'm going to show you some ways that you can improve your gardening with upcycling.

ANYTHING CAN BE A PLANT POT

Just about anything can be upcycled into a plant pot as long as it can hold soil. Check out some of the upcycling projects I have been working on.

← PLANT POT

PLANT POT

PLANT POT

MINI GREENHOUSE

Some young plants need more heat to help them grow. You can upcycle plastic bottles by cutting off one end to make mini greenhouses.

Upcycling is great because you give new life to old things and can avoid sending them to landfill.

SMALL STEPS: UPCYCLE IN YOUR GARDEN

If you want to learn more about Upcycling and Recycling, check out Morrison's book!

Becoming a Champion of Change

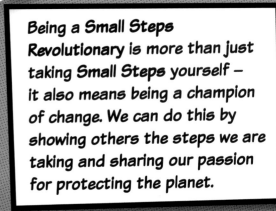

Being a Small Steps Revolutionary is more than just taking Small Steps yourself – it also means being a champion of change. We can do this by showing others the steps we are taking and sharing our passion for protecting the planet.

RAISING AWARENESS

There are lots of ways that you can raise awareness as a Small Steps Revolutionary. Some revolutionaries use social media to share their message. Recruit an adult you trust to help you use social media.

You could start a gardening club where you and your friends share ideas and work together.

Look for places that you can make a change. Are there any **Small Steps** that could help your school to make less waste? Is there an area that could be turned into a vegetable garden?

Be the change you want to see.

I worked with my teachers and classmates to make a vegetable garden and now we grow some of the food used in our school lunches.

Small Steps Revolutionaries are proud to make a change!

Share your successes with the hashtag #smallstepsrevolution

Remember, some people might not have met anyone making the changes you are making, so be nice when you talk about green gardening. People are more likely to try to make a change themselves if you are helpful instead of being mean to them – this is the **Small Steps** way!

SMALL STEPS: SHARE YOUR SUCCESSES

Ethical Living

Green gardening is only one part of the Small Steps Revolution, so what does it mean to be a Small Steps Revolutionary? It means living ethically – living the best life you can. To live ethically you need to think about the effect your actions have on the world around you.

Making the change through green gardening is not easy and won't happen overnight. Remember the golden rule: Small Steps Lead to Big Change. Focus on making small changes that you can keep to every day; every small step will take you closer to helping the environment by composting and gardening.

A good way to guide your actions as a Small Steps Revolutionary is to live by the 5 Rs. They are:

REFUSE – BEFORE YOU BUY SOMETHING, THINK HARD ABOUT WHETHER YOU NEED IT OR NOT. IF YOU DON'T, THEN REFUSE TO BUY OR ACCEPT IT.

REDUCE – SOME THINGS YOU WILL NOT BE ABLE TO REFUSE, BUT YOU CAN USE LESS. THIS WILL MEAN YOU CREATE LESS WASTE.

REUSE – BEFORE YOU THROW SOMETHING AWAY, THINK ABOUT WHETHER THAT THING CAN BE USED AGAIN. ONLY REPLACE SOMETHING IF IT CAN'T BE USED AGAIN.

REPURPOSE – THIS IS ANOTHER WAY OF SAYING UPCYCLE. IF YOU CAN, FIND A NEW WAY TO USE SOMETHING INSTEAD OF THROWING IT AWAY.

RECYCLE – IF YOU CAN'T DO ANY OF THESE THINGS THEN YOU SHOULD TRY TO RECYCLE. MAKE SURE THAT WHAT YOU PUT INTO YOUR RECYCLING BIN CAN BE RECYCLED BY YOUR LOCAL RECYCLING CENTRE.

Manifesto

THE COMPOSTING AND GARDENING MANIFESTO

- GROW YOUR KNOWLEDGE
- MEASURE YOUR CARBON FOOTPRINT
- GROW PLANTS FOR THE ANIMALS IN YOUR GARDEN
- ADD BIRD BOXES, BUG HOTELS AND PONDS TO YOUR GARDEN
- GROW SOME WEEDS
- USE ORGANIC PESTICIDES
- COMPOST YOUR ORGANIC WASTE
- COLLECT RAINWATER
- MULCH YOUR FLOWERBEDS
- USE GREY WATER TO WATER YOUR PLANTS
- GROW YOUR OWN VEGETABLES
- UPCYCLE IN YOUR GARDEN
- SHARE YOUR SUCCESSES

You are now a full member of the **Small Steps Revolution.** Keep on taking small, <u>sustainable</u> steps, spreading the word and inspiring others to do the same. Together we can and will **Save the World.**

Glossary

ATMOSPHERE	a mixture of gases that surround the Earth
CARBON DIOXIDE	a colourless gas that adds to climate change
CHEMICALS	substances that materials are made from
CLIMATE CRISIS	serious problems being caused by changes to the world's weather, caused by humans and the release of greenhouse gases into the environment
EDIBLE	can be eaten
ENRICH	to make better, stronger and more valuable
ENVIRONMENT	all the things that make up the natural world
EVAPORATING	when a liquid turns into a gas
GENERATING	making or producing
HARVEST	collect to be used for something
NUTRIENTS	natural substances that are needed for plants to grow
ORGANIC WASTE	a type of waste that is made up of natural things such as food
PESTICIDES	chemicals or substances that are used to stop or kill pests
PESTS	animals or insects that have a harmful effect on humans or the food they eat
QUALITY	how good something is
RECRUIT	to bring a member into a group
RELIABLE	trusted
RESOURCES	the things used to make something
SUSTAINABLE	able to be used without damaging future generations
SYSTEM	a series of things that are connected and work together
UPCYCLE	when an old or broken thing is turned into something new and more valuable

Index